TSUNAMIS

by Jennifer Swanson

Content Consultant
Stephen A. Nelson
Associate Professor of Geology
Tulane University

CORE
LIBRARY

Published by ABDO Publishing Company, PO Box 398166, Minneapolis, MN 55439. Copyright © 2014 by Abdo Consulting Group, Inc. International copyrights reserved in all countries. No part of this book may be reproduced in any form without written permission from the publisher. The Core Library™ is a trademark and logo of ABDO Publishing Company.

Printed in the United States of America,
North Mankato, Minnesota
052013
092013

Editor: Lauren Coss
Series Designer: Becky Daum

Library of Congress Control Number: 2013932502

Cataloging-in-Publication Data
Swanson, Jennifer.
 Tsunamis / Jennifer Swanson.
   p. cm. -- (Earth in action)
ISBN 978-1-61783-941-2 (lib. bdg.)
ISBN 978-1-62403-006-2 (pbk.)
1. Tsunamis--Juvenile literature. 2. Natural disasters--Juvenile literature. I. Title.
551.46--dc23

                                        2013932502

Photo Credits: JIJI Press/AFP/Getty Images, cover, 1; Kyodo News/AP Images, 4, 45; AP Images, 6; Kamaishi Port Office/Kyodo News/AP Images, 8; Tomiuri Shimbun/AP Images, 10; Yasushi Kanno/Yomiuri Shimbun/AP Images, 12; Thinkstock, 14, 32; Red Line Editorial, 17, 36; Warren Goldswain/Shutterstock Images, 19; Bryant Anderson/AP Images, 21; Gemunu Amarasinghe/AP Images, 22; Mary Plage/Getty Images, 24; Luciano Corbella/Dorling Kindersley, 26; Greg Baker/AP Images, 29; Rob Griffith/AP Images, 30; Eugene Tanner/AP Images, 34; Shutterstock Images, 36; Rick Bowmer/AP Images, 37; Don Ryan/AP Images, 39; Sipa USA/AP Images, 40

CONTENTS

CHAPTER ONE

COASTAL TERROR

The afternoon of March 11, 2011, Saeko Kudo was at home with her mother in Kamaishi, Northern Japan. Suddenly the floor started shaking. It was a very strong earthquake. Small earthquakes had been happening often in the past two days. But this one was different. The shaking kept going on. It got stronger. Earthquakes did not normally last this long.

On March 11, 2011, a powerful earthquake triggered a massive tsunami that devastated much of northern Japan.

Tsunami waves can flood coastal areas for miles inland.

The Tsunami Rushes In

About 30 minutes after the initial shaking, Saeko looked out the window. Saeko lived on the coast. She noticed the water in the harbor was much lower than usual. Soon, the water disappeared completely. She knew something was very wrong. It was time for Saeko and her mother to leave—now!

By the time Saeko helped her mother outside, the water had returned to the harbor. It was flowing very fast toward the shore and spilling over the seawall. Within

Holding Back the Tide

Construction on a huge wall, called a breakwater, in the bay outside Kamaishi was completed in 2009. It was built to reduce the impact of tsunami strikes. At more than 207 feet (63 m) high, the heavy concrete wall was built on the floor of the bay. It stood 25 feet (8 m) above waterline and was 1.2 miles (1.9 km) long. The wall cost $1.5 billion to build. Still, it was no match for the more than 14-foot (4-m) waves from the 2011 tsunami. The force of the waves pounded the wall to pieces in a matter of minutes. Then the water rushed into Kamaishi.

A reporter in Kamaishi was swept away by the 2011 tsunami. He was lucky to survive with only minor injuries.

minutes, the water was coming through their door and flooding the house. Saeko and her mother went back inside the house and up to the second floor. The water continued pouring into their home. Soon it was level with the window on the second floor. Saeko and her mother climbed out onto the roof. The fierce wall of water continued rising. Soon the water engulfed them.

Saeko had been clinging to part of the roof. She knew the only way to survive was to let go and try to float to the very peak of the house. Saeko floated to the top of the roof and grabbed onto the tiles.

A Giant Quake

Like most other tsunamis, an earthquake caused the 2011 Japan tsunami. The earth's crust is made up of many pieces of land, called plates. The plates move very slowly. They pull away from, push toward, or slide past one another. Sometimes when two plates collide or slide past one another, an earthquake happens. Earthquakes under the ocean can create tsunamis. The 2011 earthquake was the fifth largest in the world. It was the strongest ever to hit Japan.

After the 2011 tsunami, the waters were still so high that many rescuers had to use boats to pick up survivors.

She reached down and helped her mother up to the top of the roof.

Together they clung to the tip of their house as the raging waters swirled around them. They hung on for 30 minutes, until the water levels began to fall. Saeko and her mother were lucky. They had survived one of the most devastating tsunamis Japan had ever seen.

Deadly Waves

A tsunami is a single, large wave or a series of large waves in the ocean. Also known as a seismic sea wave, most tsunamis are caused by underwater earthquakes. Tsunamis can happen along coasts all around the world. But they are most common in the Pacific Ocean.

The March 2011 tsunami devastated northern Japan. In some places, the wave was three stories high. It wiped out houses, cars, trains, and businesses. Thousands of people were killed instantly by drowning or by being struck by debris. Others were swept

The tsunami waves that hit Japan caused massive and widespread destruction.

out to sea. The tsunami caused massive flooding, destroying crops, buildings, and other property. All told, more than 15,000 people lost their lives.

Tsunamis are one of nature's most deadly forces. The deeper the water, the faster tsunamis move. At more than 500 miles per hour (800 km/h), a tsunami wave can travel as fast as an airplane. The energy that tsunamis generate is enormous. In fact, the energy of the tsunami that hit Japan in 2011 was nearly equal to the amount of energy that New York City uses in a week.

Saeko Kudo described her frightening experience during the Japanese tsunami in a 2011 documentary:

> The water level fell drastically. There was water in the harbor, but when I looked again, it was gone. I could see the black mud on the ocean floor. I realized this was no ordinary tsunami. It was definitely going to come over the wall. I realized this, so I shouted, "Let's get out of here!". . . At first, it just came over the wall, just as high as the wall. It wasn't a giant wave that hit all at once; it was a gradual swell that came over the wall. The moment I saw it come over, there was water at my feet. So we ran up to the second floor of the house.

> Source: Surviving the Tsunami. *Nova.* WGBH Educational Foundation, September 28, 2011. Transcript. Web. Accessed April 10, 2013.

Consider Your Audience

Read this passage closely. Saeko was interviewed for a documentary. How would you adapt Saeko's words for a different format and audience? Write a blog post conveying the information in the passage to this new audience. How is your blog post different from the original passage?

CHAPTER TWO

BIRTH OF A KILLER WAVE

Tsunamis are different from regular ocean waves that ripple through the water every day. Regular waves are caused by wind or tides. Wind-driven waves travel in a circular motion. They push water up onto the beach and then retreat quickly into the ocean. Tidal waves are caused by the pull of the moon and the sun. The waves of a tsunami, however, are much deeper. They extend thousands of feet under

Most large ocean waves are caused by wind or tides. These don't cause the same damage as the tsunamis that sometimes hit land.

water. The waves move away from the tsunami source in all directions. Earthquakes, underwater volcanic eruptions, landslides, or even meteorites that fall into the ocean from the sky can cause tsunamis.

Tsunamis can happen anywhere in the world. But more than 70 percent of tsunamis happen in the Pacific Ocean. The Pacific Ocean covers more than one-third of the earth. It is the largest body of water on the planet.

Earthquake-Caused Tsunamis

Earthquakes cause most tsunamis. Earthquakes release huge amounts of

Ring of Fire

The Pacific plate lies under the Pacific Ocean. Around the boundaries of the Pacific plate, large mountains and deep trenches have formed. This area is known as the Ring of Fire. It is a geologically active place where the Pacific plate collides with, slides past, and pulls away from nearby plates. This activity causes many earthquakes and volcanoes. More tsunamis occur in and around the Ring of Fire than in any other region in the world. Shifting plates also cause tsunamis in the Mediterranean Sea, the Caribbean Sea, the Atlantic Ocean, and the Indian Ocean.

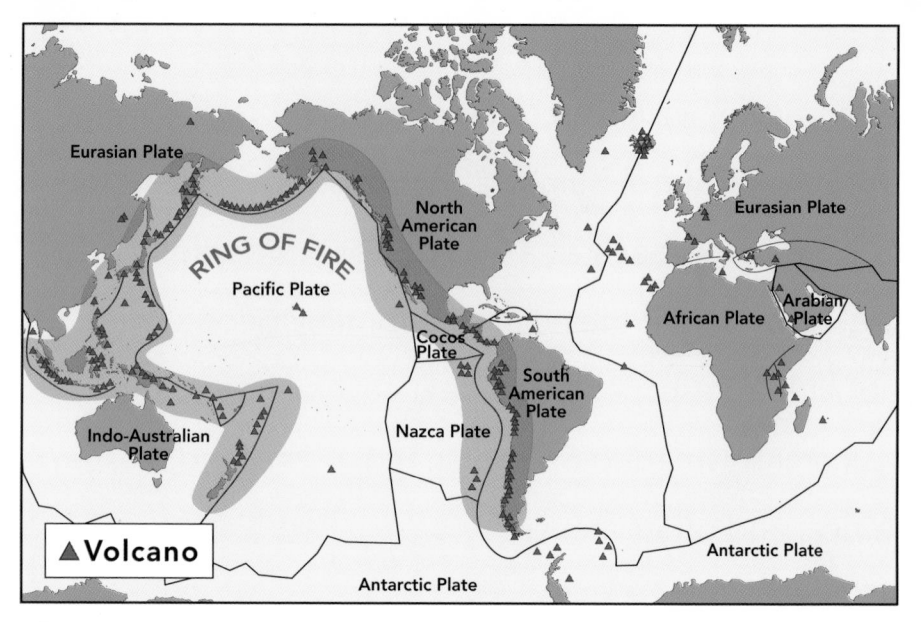

The Ring of Fire

This diagram shows the geography of the Ring of Fire. After reading about the Ring of Fire, what did you imagine it would look like? How has your vision changed? How does seeing the diagram of the Ring of Fire help you better understand how the movement of the Pacific plate can create a tsunami?

energy. When the ocean floor shifts in an earthquake, the energy pushes up on the water above it. This forms a wave.

On December 26, 2004, a 9.3-magnitude earthquake struck near the island nation of Indonesia. The earthquake triggered a huge tsunami. This tsunami affected more than 18 countries and killed approximately 300,000 people. Within minutes of the

earthquake, waves up to 80 feet (24 m) high crashed onto the island of Sumatra. Witnesses described the tsunami's approach as a wall of water. People fled to higher ground if they could. But many people were not able to escape. In the next several hours, the tsunami traveled to Sri Lanka, India, Thailand, eastern Africa, and other areas.

Volcanoes

Volcanoes can also cause massive tsunamis. When an underwater volcano or a volcanic island erupts, debris and parts of the volcano itself explode or collapse into the water. This can trigger a tsunami.

One of the most destructive tsunamis in history occurred when the volcano on the Indonesian island of Krakatau erupted. The violent explosion destroyed most of the island and created a series of tsunamis. Some of the waves were more than 120 feet (37 m) tall. That is as high as a 12-story building. The tsunami killed more than 30,000 people on the nearby islands of Java and Sumatra. The tsunami was so huge,

The Krakatau volcano has erupted in more recent years without causing another massive tsunami.

Great Travelers

Tsunamis can strike far from the triggering earthquake, volcanic eruption, or landslide. The 2011 earthquake near Japan created distant waves that sped across the Pacific Ocean. Less than eight hours after the earthquake, a tsunami hit the Hawaiian Islands. Six-foot (1.8-m) waves swamped the island of Maui, more than 3,800 miles (6,116 km) from the earthquake's epicenter. The waves continued on to the coast of California, where they caused an 8-foot (2.4-m) water surge at Crescent City, California. Crescent City is more than 6,000 miles (9,656 km) from the point where the earthquake happened.

its waves stretched all the way to the English Channel. This is halfway around the world from Krakatau.

Danger: Falling Rocks

Tsunamis are sometimes triggered by landslides. Landslide-caused tsunamis are especially common in fjords. A fjord is a long, narrow inlet of ocean. High mountains often surround the inlet. Pieces of rocks regularly break off and plunge into the water. Large rock pieces can send a tsunami out into the ocean.

A boat fights through tsunami waves off the coast of Crescent City, California. The waves were triggered by Japan's 2011 earthquake.

On July 9, 1958, an earthquake caused huge chunks of rock to break off the side of a coastal mountain in Lituya Bay, Alaska. The falling rock crashed into the ocean, displacing massive amounts of water. The resulting tsunami created a wave more than 1,720 feet (524 m) tall. It smashed into the other side of the bay and sent a wave 394 feet (120 m) tall racing toward the ocean at 100 miles per hour

Tsunami waves flood houses along the coast of Sri Lanka in 2004.

(160 km/h). Lituya Bay is very isolated, so not many people were affected by this event.

Meteorites striking the water can also trigger tsunamis. No meteorites have been large enough to create a tsunami in recent history. But many scientists believe a meteorite impact near Mexico 65 million years ago may have caused huge tsunamis. This same meteorite may be one of the reasons dinosaurs went extinct.

Seventeen-year-old Thrishana Pothupitiya was living in Sri Lanka when the tsunami hit on December 26, 2004. She was so moved by the devastation and the people who came to the aid of the tsunami's victims, that she wrote a poem titled "Tsunami You Hit My Island Home":

. . .

From far away people came
To lend a helping hand
Humanity poured through the veins
Of every man and child.

The Tsunami which hit our land
On "Uduwap" poya day
Has freed us from ourselves
Has shown us the correct way.

. . .

What's the Big Idea?

Take a close look at this poem. What is Thrishana trying to say about how the tsunami affected her country? Do you think she feels it was a positive event or a negative event? What do you think she means by the phrase "Has freed us from ourselves"?

CHAPTER THREE

TSUNAMI PHASES

There are four phases of tsunami formation. The first phase is called initiation. In the initiation phase, a force disturbs the water. For example, two plates in the ocean floor shift or an underwater volcano erupts. This abrupt movement of the water causes a huge wave to form.

The second phase of formation is called the split. Here, the tsunami splits into two waves. The waves

A volcanic eruption under or near the ocean can cause tsunami initiation.

Most tsunamis begin when an undersea earthquake causes a disturbance underwater.

move away from each other in opposite directions. Waves have two parts: a crest and trough. The crest is the highest part of the wave, and the trough is the lowest. One wave, called the distant tsunami, travels out into the deep ocean. The distant tsunami can have a wavelength, or distance between wave crests, up to 300 miles (483 km) long. It can extend hundreds of miles under the ocean. Most of these long, deep waves are less than three feet (1 m) tall. That is just a little higher than the average school desk. The second wave heads toward the nearest piece of land. This wave is known as the local tsunami.

Moving Toward Shore

The third phase of tsunami formation is called amplification. During this phase, the local tsunami slows down as it encounters the shallow sea floor. Some of the energy pushing the wave forward is directed upward. This makes the height of the wave amplify, or increase. That is why the wave of a tsunami is so high when it hits land. Sometimes the trough of the wave hits before the crest. When this happens, the water may recede before the crest

Tsunami Zone

Tsunamis often strike the same areas again and again. All of the people in the tiny village of Aneyoshi, Japan, survived the 2011 tsunami because they listened to the warnings of their ancestors. Stone blocks were placed on hillsides more than 100 years ago. Legend states villagers should not build their houses below these markers. The legend says if houses stay above the marker, they will be safe from a tsunami. It worked. When the 2011 tsunami hit the village of Aneyoshi, the waters remained 300 feet (91 m) below the markers.

of the wave strikes. Other times the crest strikes first. Then the water will flood onshore with no warning.

The fourth stage of tsunami formation is called the run-up. In this phase, the water from the tsunami surges onto shore. Water comes on shore in one of two ways. Most tsunamis flood the shore like a very large tide. This makes the ocean look like it is slowly rising. Other tsunamis form a bore, or a vertical wall of water, as they come ashore.

Phase four can last for hours. In fact, the first wave of the run-up may not be the largest wave. Once the first wave hits during the run-up, the energy from the wave reflects back into the ocean. This increase in

Nuclear Meltdown

The widespread flooding during the March 2011 tsunami affected one of Japan's nuclear power plants. Fukushima Plant 1 lost power because of the excess water. Seawater from the tsunami had flooded the backup generators, so they did not work. Radiation began leaking outside the plant. Thousands of people were evacuated from their homes.

Even after the water goes down, it can take months or even years for life to return to normal in areas affected by a tsunami.

energy can cause even higher waves to form. After the tsunami rushes onto land, it loses momentum. Then water rushes back toward the sea, dragging debris, people, animals, and other objects with it.

The Aftermath

Tsunamis can demolish everything in their path. Buildings may be toppled, houses destroyed, and cars swept out to sea. Bridges can be carried away or

Red Cross workers helped victims by providing food and supplies after a tsunami struck the Pacific Ocean's Solomon Islands in 2007.

knocked off their bases due to the massive force of a tsunami. Tsunamis can cause flooding many miles inland. Tsunamis can push water into rivers or lakes. It can take days for the water to recede out to sea.

Drinking water may be contaminated by seawater from the tsunami. Crops can be destroyed in the

flooding. Tsunamis often knock down power lines or flood power plants. Houses and schools may be destroyed, so people have nowhere to live or take shelter. When tsunamis happen, international organizations, such as the Red Cross and the Salvation Army, provide aid. They bring food, water, and clothing to disaster areas. Countries not affected by the tsunamis send help in the form of money and supplies. Volunteers help clean up and rebuild. But this can take months or years.

CHAPTER FOUR

WARNING: TSUNAMI APPROACHING

Tsunamis have been responsible for thousands of deaths over the past 500 years or more. Once a tsunami forms, there is no way to stop it. However, warning people when a tsunami is on its way can give them time to get to safety.

Warning Centers

Two tsunami-warning centers have been set up to track tsunami formation. The West Coast and Alaska

In places where tsunamis are common, signs warn people to move to higher ground quickly if they feel an earthquake.

Scientists at the Pacific Tsunami Warning Center predict and track tsunamis.

Tsunami Warning Center is responsible for alerting both the east and west coasts of the United States and Canada about incoming tsunamis. The Pacific Tsunami Warning Center provides information to all of the countries in and near the Pacific Ocean. There is no warning center in the Atlantic Ocean, so the Pacific Tsunami Warning Center also monitors countries in the Indian Ocean and the Caribbean Sea.

Scientists on Alert

Scientists are able to record underwater earthquakes, the main cause of most tsunamis. They use

seismographs to record when and where earthquakes strike. If a large underwater earthquake strikes, scientists know the tsunami risk is high for nearby coasts.

Tracking earthquakes alone is not enough to predict a tsunami. Changes in the ocean surface also tell scientists a great deal about tsunamis. Scientists developed the Deep-ocean Assessment and Reporting of Tsunamis (DART) system in 1995. The DART is a series of cables crisscrossing the floors of the world's oceans. These cables sense when a large wave,

Seismographs

A seismograph is a simple instrument. The bottom base is attached to the ground. The top part has an arm with a heavy metal weight hanging from it. The metal weight hangs freely, meaning it can move back and forth. A pen is attached to the bottom of the weight. During an earthquake, the ground shakes. This causes the metal weight to swing. As the weight moves, the pen travels back and forth on a piece of paper. The scratchings from the pen give information about the earthquake. These scratchings tell scientists the size and location of the earthquake.

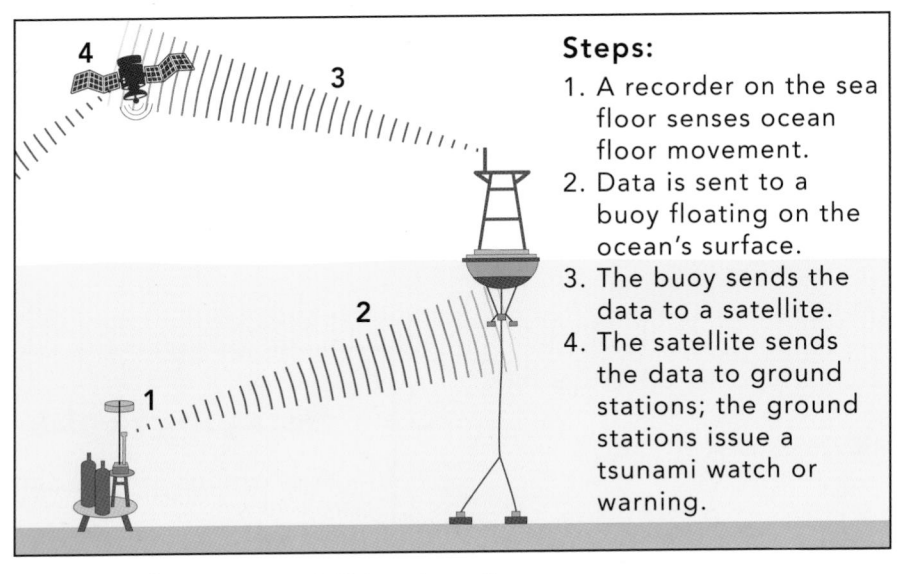

Steps:

1. A recorder on the sea floor senses ocean floor movement.
2. Data is sent to a buoy floating on the ocean's surface.
3. The buoy sends the data to a satellite.
4. The satellite sends the data to ground stations; the ground stations issue a tsunami watch or warning.

The Pacific Tsunami Warning System

This diagram shows how the Pacific Tsunami Warning Center's system works. After reading about how scientists track tsunamis, were you surprised by how this system looks? How does seeing the warning system in place help you better understand how scientists gather information?

such as a tsunami, passes over them. The information is then sent to a buoy floating on the surface of the ocean. Finally, the information makes its way to a tidal station. Scientists at the tidal station use the information to look for a nearby earthquake as the source.

Satellites are used to track wave heights and wave speeds across the ocean. When scientists

Coastal schools hold tsunami drills so students can practice what to do if a tsunami strikes.

discover a low wave traveling very quickly, they watch it closely to see if it is a tsunami.

Scientists use computer models to try to figure out where the tsunami will travel. When they have an idea of the tsunami track, warnings are sent to the countries in its path. It can take up to an hour to gather all the information and issue a warning. When the warning finally comes, people must take immediate action.

Many people living in tsunami zones know to move to higher ground when they feel an earthquake

Head for High Ground!

There are four levels of notification for the tsunami warning system:

Tsunami Information/ Bulletin: This warning means an earthquake has happened nearby. Nearby areas should remain alert.

Tsunami Watch: This warning is issued to countries near the earthquake. These areas should be prepared to activate warnings systems if needed.

Tsunami Advisory: This warning is issued to countries in the direct path of a possible tsunami, should one form.

Tsunami Warning: This warning means there is a tsunami on its way. People should head to high ground immediately.

shake the ground. If a tsunami's source is far away, people may have no idea it is coming. When a region receives a tsunami alert from one of the warning centers, officials may issue a watch, an advisory, or a warning. A warning is the most serious alert. Many coastal towns have warning sirens to alert residents that a tsunami is coming.

People who live near the coast and feel an earthquake should not wait for the tsunami warning to move to higher ground. The

The ocean water receded, revealing bare beach before the big tsunami waves hit Japan in March 2011.

tsunami could arrive before officials have time to issue the warning. If there is time, people should move to the top of the nearest hill or building. If there is not enough time to evacuate, people should climb to the highest point in their house.

Receding water is a sign a tsunami is coming. This means the trough, or low part, of the wave has reached shore. The rest of the wave will follow soon.

People should not stand along the shore to watch for the tsunami. By the time the wave can be seen, it is too late to move out of its path. No one can outrun

Residents of Oahu, Hawaii, moved to higher ground after a tsunami warning was issued in 2010.

a tsunami. Even if the first wave is shallow, people need to remain alert. A tsunami is often a series of waves. The highest waves could still be on their way. It can take hours for all of a tsunami's waves to come ashore. People should not return to the shore until all the waves have come in.

Predicting for the Future

Scientists continue to improve early warning techniques. New computer systems are being developed. They analyze data from scientists,

EXPLORE ONLINE

The focus of Chapter Four is the detection and prevention of tsunamis. This chapter also touches on the use of satellites and computers to predict tsunamis. The Web site below focuses on a different part of tsunami prediction. As you know, every source is different. How is the information provided on the Web site different from the information in Chapter Four? What information, if any, is the same? How do the two sources present information differently? What can you learn from this Web site?

Tsunami Prediction

www.mycorelibrary.com/tsunamis

as well as a variety of other details, including coastline size, shape, depth, and historical data. This information helps scientists make the most accurate predictions possible. These new systems could help save many lives.

For many people who live along coastlines, tsunamis are a fact of life. Sooner or later, another tsunami will likely occur. Tsunamis cannot be stopped, but with good warning systems and evacuation plans, people can survive them.

TEN DEADLY TSUNAMIS

September 20, 1498
Enshunada Sea, Japan
This magnitude 8.3 earthquake generated huge destructive tsunami waves along the coast of Japan. Approximately 31,000 people died.

January 18, 1586
Ise Bay, Japan
Caused by an 8.2-magnitude earthquake, this tsunami was approximately 19 feet (6 m) high. It completely wiped out the town of Nagahama, Japan, and killed 8,000 people.

October 28, 1707
Nankaido, Japan
Caused by an 8.4-magnitude earthquake, the tsunami was as high as 82 feet (25 m). Approximately 30,000 people died in the tsunami.

November 1, 1755
Lisbon, Portugal
An 8.5-magnitude earthquake caused a tsunami with three large waves approximately 100 feet (30 m) high. More than 60,000 people died in Portugal, Morocco, and Spain.

April 24, 1771
Ryuku Islands, Japan
Caused by an earthquake of magnitude 7.4, this tsunami reached approximately 49 feet (15 m) high. It affected many of the islands surrounding Japan and killed nearly 12,000 people.

August 13, 1868
Northern Chile
Caused by two earthquakes, both of magnitude 8.5, the tsunami was about 68 feet (21 m) high. The waves lasted for almost three days and killed 25,000 people.

August 27, 1883

Krakatau, Indonesia

Caused by a volcanic explosion, the tsunami had several waves of 121 feet (37 m) high. It destroyed part of the island of Krakatau. More than 36,000 people were killed on nearby islands.

June 15, 1896

Sanriku, Japan

A 7.6-magnitude earthquake triggered a tsunami that reached a height of 125 feet (38 m). The distant wave traveled to China, where it killed 4,000 people.

December 26, 2004

Sumatra, Indonesia

Caused by a 9.1-magnitude earthquake, the tsunami was 164 feet (50 m) tall. Approximately 230,000 people died in the disaster.

March 11, 2011

North Pacific Coast, Japan

Caused by a 9.0-magnitude earthquake, this tsunami was 32 feet (10 m) high. It disrupted nuclear power plants in the area, releasing radiation into the atmosphere.

Dig Deeper

After reading this book, what questions do you still have about tsunamis? Do you want to learn more about how scientists track and predict them? Maybe you want to know why tsunamis happen in the first place. Write down one or two questions that can guide you in your research. With an adult's help, find reliable sources to help answer your questions. Write a few sentences about how you did your research and what you learned from it.

You Are There

This book discusses what a tsunami does when it reaches land. Imagine you are on the island of Japan, and the tsunami warning sirens have just been sounded. What will you do? Will you react immediately or wait and see what happens? Will you go with your parents in a car to evacuate or head to the nearest high ground on foot? How do you think others will react to the warning sirens?

Say What?

Studying tsunamis can mean learning a lot of new vocabulary. Find five words in this book you have never read before. Use a dictionary to find out what they mean. Then write the meanings in your own words, and use each word in a new sentence.

Why Do I Care?

Tsunamis rarely affect the United States. Still people in coastal areas should be prepared. How does learning about tsunamis and how they form help you better understand them? How does being ready for a tsunami help you prepare for other natural disasters?

GLOSSARY

bore
tsunami that forms a vertical wall of water

crest
the highest point of a wave

distant wave
half of the original tsunami wave that heads out into the ocean

epicenter
the point on the earth's surface above the place from which the shock waves of an earthquake radiate

fjord
a long, narrow inlet of sea bordered by cliffs

local tsunami
half of the original tsunami wave that heads toward the nearest shoreline

magnitude
the measure of the size of the earthquake based on the energy released

meteorite
a body of matter from space that enters the atmosphere and lands on the earth

seismograph
an instrument for measuring and recording the vibrations of earthquakes

trough
the lowest point of a wave

wavelength
the distance between the peak of one wave and the peak of the next wave

LEARN MORE

Books

Hamilton, John. *Tsunamis.* Edina, MN: ABDO, 2006.

Walker, Niki. *Tsunami Alert.* New York: Crabtree, 2006.

Wendorff, Anne. *Tsunamis.* New York: Scholastic, 2008.

Web Links

To learn more about tsunamis, visit ABDO Publishing Company online at **www.abdopublishing.com**. Web sites about tsunamis are featured on our Book Links page. These links are routinely monitored and updated to provide the most current information available.

Visit **www.mycorelibrary.com** for free additional tools for teachers and students.

INDEX

ABOUT THE AUTHOR

Jennifer Swanson's first love is science. She is the author of nine nonfiction books for kids. When not writing, Swanson can be found walking along the beach looking for seashells and studying the waves.